B A K A TAROT

BAKA

TAROT

The Fool's Calligraphic Journey

Camelia Elias

Baka Tarot: The Fool's Calligraphic Journey © Camelia Elias 2023.
Published by EyeCorner Press in August 2023, Denmark.
Designed and typeset by Camelia Elias.
Baka Tarot & calligraphy illustrations by Camelia Elias.

ISBN 978-87-92633-17-0

www.eyecorner.press

CONTENTS

A CALLIGRAPHIC JOURNEY

The Scribe

B aka Tarot is the result of a moment of regret. As I was looking one day at some calligraphy art and scrolls I made, I realized that it had been too long since I last had a rendezvous with a brush. I did not have the time to go through a proper calligraphy session, but I thought that if I combined real black ink with digital ink, I might get something done. As I didn't want to linger on past achievements, I decided to do something about my regret. Exorcise it by creating something again.

I already had a method. As any creation of a deck of cards follows a tight principle I developed years ago, one that I call, *One Cut, One Blood,* I gave myself the time it takes to do all the cards in just one sitting. At some point I lost my nerve. How does one draw a trumpet, calligraphy style? As I couldn't make up my mind, I thought I'd go for a clarinet instead. You can see it on the Judgment card here.

In addition to the 22 traditional trumps in a tarot pack, I created 4 extra cards from the world of poker. I named them after the actions in the game: Call, Check, Raise, and Fold. I could just imagine the usefulness of such words in divination, especially when advice is needed: do we risk it, or do we fold it? So far I've had great results using these cards. They complement the trumps of the tarot to the letter. It was a good idea to add them to the pack. After all, what we do with the cards and the way we create them is forever subject to chance. If this wasn't the case, we wouldn't be able to appreciate the ludic in life. *Baka*, the Japanese word for Fool, participates in this game, also as an homage to a long, calligraphic tradition.

THE TALISMAN

Although I created this deck entirely for my own pleasure, when I shared in public a few images from it, people started coveting it. Coveting is bad, so I decided to indulge. I set out to make 22 sets of cards, hand cut them, sand and bone their edges, and bleed in the process.

I didn't mind my fingers getting busted, as such an ordeal is part of the magic and what goes into the creation of a talisman.

While I was at it, I went from experiencing the joy of making a special thing to cursing like a true Gypsy from Romania. But all of this is part of the enchantment. For a whole week I worked intensely at it to the point where I forgot to eat. Or when I was offered food, I got annoyed. All very silly, really, but then this tarot is called *Baka Tarot,* the *baka* in it suggesting everything irrational that goes into creating something unconventional.

My own sister said, 'what a foolish thing, to spend so much time on this,' and I couldn't agree more. But from the perspective of magic, I was with a different logic there. I was with the logic of how love triumphs, the love of beauty, poetry, and art.

Baka Tarot was released in this limited edition on August 17, 2023. The deck was accompanied by a personalized black ink sigil inside a title card that also featured a QR code to a text on my website describing the cards. This text formed the basis for the book you're reading now, a book that invites you to encounter the 26 cards, as they tell both an individual story and a story in a different context. As each description of the 26 cards culminates in a short reading of a 3-card string, you get a sense of how the *baka* moves, so to speak, what risks the fool takes, and what fortunes he encounters. Along the way you will notice that on most of the cards there is all sorts of 'writing on the wall' in the form of asemic script, or writing that carries no semantic significance. It's all gobbledygook, but there's a reason for it.

As I like to think of this deck as carrying talismanic power, it follows the tradition for crafting spells that have a declarative nature. For instance, you will note that the word *abracadabra* appears in connection with the description of several cards. *Baka Tarot* uses this type of magical invocation in order to function as a key that opens secret doors. As with all things tarot, if we didn't traffic with *some* secrets, we would not be nearly as fascinating in our endeavors to see the world from the perspective of having our habitual patterns of thinking derailed, so that we might consider novel approaches to whatever we may happen to sit with.

The first edition of *Baka Tarot* was crafted as part of a ritual. Besides the object itself that was infused with specific incantations during the process of making it, suffumigation was also performed in accordance with having observed the proper planetary alignments, drawing down just the stellar power for the cards. Although a second edition now exists in standard form, printed by the fine company, *Make Playing Cards* or MPC, making the *Baka Tarot* accessible to all who want it, the cards you're looking at in this book come from my prototype deck, the talisman created for a magical purpose, for that's how this *baka* rolls.

Enjoy meeting the cards and reading about them. The intention behind the 26 fragments of narrative here is to offer both a familiar story and one that's surprising, the familiar story being applicable to reading with other tarots as well. But the magic is in the nature of calligraphy to always surprise the eye and then inflect the narrative voice about what is seen in unexpected ways. Each stroke is informed by a silent *abracadabra,* but because silent, all the more powerful.

Baka Tarot tells the story of this silent act, in the process reminding us of how flexible our hips were once upon a time, when we would also swing in our own hola hoops, grinning wholeheartedly.

THE FOOL

The Fool

Any shape the Fool sits on is his throne. On this throne the Fool carries himself with a confidence all his own. No one else gets this confidence, as most people act in accordance with consecrated societal rules. So the general attitude towards the Fool is one of judgment and dismay, 'how can he...?' *'Baka,'* the Japanese go, shaking their heads, thus sharing a universal response to the Fool's behavior: 'anything but this...' Yet the Fool lives according to his own rules, his chief signature being indifference. What is unacceptable to all is the joy of the Fool, his pain and his sorrow. Yet, since the Fool doesn't care about anything, his thoughtlessness, improvidence, and negligence render him an unreliable subject.

In *Baka Tarot,* if this Fool looks like a king, it's because he sits in a hula hoop ring. Swinging this ring around his hips requires great coordination skills. Sitting on the edge of a ring is also quite dangerous. Fun too, but for how long? Like a circus monkey, while enchanting you with his free fall style of moves, the Fool is not a creature you want to live with, as he will mess with every single plan or project you may have.

As an idiot savant, however, the Fool knows the human condition best. Just look at this trio of cards here: *The Sun, The Moon & The Fool*. First the hot sun, and then the cold moon. People fall in love and feel each other's energy. Then the entropy. 'What attracted us to begin with?' they ask, when they end up misunderstanding one another, now each turning to their own private dreams. This the Fool can observe, and then say, 'what a foolish dream love is,' and who can argue with that?

If the Fool appears deep and profound in his countenance here, it's because of the magnifying glass that hangs from his neck. But he is not using it to conduct experiments in science. He uses it as a mirror. Looking at his own distorted face in it, the Fool becomes involuntarily aware of all the folly in the world. Some Fools walk around shouting: 'everything is holy.' Our *Baka* here goes, 'everything is folly, and I am its embodiment.' This we can see for ourselves, as we note that the Fool is already inside the very thing he is looking into.

When the wisdom of the Fool strikes, we're left with a sense of having glimpsed the void, without getting lost in it.

The Sun

The Moon

The Fool

THE MAGICIAN

The Magician

In the Magician's hands the Fool's hula hoop can take any shape. A calligraphist magician would say, 'this is my *ensō*, my beginning without end, and my end without beginning.' No one can grasp paradoxes better than the Magician, since he is the one who lives with contradictions. He dedicates his life to the prestige, the perfect magic trick that makes us go admiringly, 'how could he do that?' 'Come ye all,' he may say on stage, 'and I'll show you how I cut this woman into pieces, make your coins appear and disappear, and put you on another planet.'

We don't know what the Magician does exactly, but we like it. His signature is to manipulate with light. Stage light, that is. He is the master of switches. 'Lights on, lights off,' he instructs the lighting technician, by using magical words. *Abracadabra* and *Open Sesame* are his favorite.

'This is possible,' he says, and 'this is how you'll see it, as soon as you'll step inside the magic through this portal.' The Magician's secret weapon is manipulating with belief, the suspended kind being his own hula hoop ring. You want to be close to the Magician because he is full of clever ideas, but can you trust him? Sometimes when the Magician has a proposition, it just sounds so good, but it is also true or useful? Look at the trio of cards here: *The Empress, The Magician & High Priests.* 'You can unleash your passion,' the Magician says to the Empress, but when the High Priests gather for an exorcism, all bets are off. The Magician can perform, but can he also win at the game of who is to suppress whose lust?

Hanging from the Magician's belt is a key tied to two tassels. We can see the key, but we can't see the keyhole he is gesturing towards. He depicts it with his hand, so we have an idea. But this keyhole is not real. Or is it? As the Magician stands in a keyhole himself, we want to be convinced of his reality. But his role is not trafficking with certitude. He is into thresholds. Closing and opening doors. Who cares about the real? The only philosophy you need is the pragmatic kind: 'Fake it 'til you make it' is the key to all secrets. If we're not magicians ourselves, it's because we insist on asking the wrong question, 'but is it real?' even as we have stepped already inside the palace of our own fantasies and pleasures.

The Empress   The Magician   High Priests

THE HIGH PRIESTESS

The High Priestess

The High Priestess likes to read. When she reads about how Medusa lost her head to Perseus, her coat becomes a sea of snakes, rising as one's hair does when the story is good. The thing about sitting with good books is that they take you to another place. They allow you to try other embodiments, other skins. Books can make you shapeshift and experience what you would never, if you just sat there, performing tasks or merely staring into space.

Books, like Perseus' mirrored shield, can capture the essence of passion, the same that gets you hanged, only so that passion can then go deeper, heeding the casting of spells in the underworld, the world of demons and devils. But a High Priestess is not only invested in tales of ardor and longing. She also keeps scores. If you betray her, she'll turn you into a fish fossil or a trilobite. If she catches you by your heel, your soft Achilles' spot, she will sell your soul to the Devil.

For all her allure of a seductive mystique, the High Priestess is a terrifying being. In traditional takes on the tarot the High Priestess is seen as the embodiment of sensitivity and intuition.

But, Lord have mercy! If the High Priestess was only that, she would be half the woman she actually is. As any reader knows, a reader of books, that is, not cards, what one gets from books is the ability to feel and think at the same time. Being sensitive and at the same time being able to reason your emotions is where the magic is. This combination is the key to the praised intuition that the High Priestess possesses, to her clear vision and insight.

In a cartomantic context, this trio of cards, *The Hanged Man, The High Priestess & The Devil* tell their tale. As the ink flows and the words weave, not even the look of love can transcend the petrifying grasp of a truly cruel gaze.

If the High Priestess rolls the dice, and then performs an act of bibliomancy at chance, a whole legion will want to know the rules of her game. But will she reveal her secrets? I hear the Devil laughing.

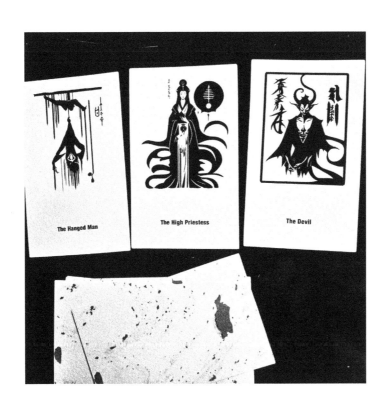

The Hanged Man   The High Priestess   The Devil

THE EMPRESS

The Empress

In most mainstream descriptions of the Empress, we find this figure associated primarily with nurturing traits. She is the mother. Now, granted, while no one is more powerful than a mother, this is not what we actually see in most tarots. What we see is a woman on a throne, or someone who dons the imperial dress. From the perspective of public function, the historical tarots got it right: no woman in power brings her children to the negotiating table. This is still the case, if we're talking about serious business, not some wishful thinking business that casts the mother as the CEO of fantasy land.

What we see in most historically accurate tarots is a representation of the Empress as a woman who acts in the public sphere. In this public office there's hardly any trace of her power in the private sphere, where she may also command over both her children and her husband. Whoever designed the first tarots decided that the intimacy of the domestic space is not the image we want to look at. Now obviously in this day and age of inclusivity, there's rejection of the idea that a woman's private business could not and should not *also* be a matter of public business, but as far as I'm concerned I like to keep it simple: either I'm looking at a mother, or I'm looking at a public ruler. If the latter, then I want my words about the ruler to match that image.

Therefore I suggest that if this card shows up in your readings, you refrain from imposing on the Empress nurturing qualities. She may possess them, but that's not what we see. Her dress and demeanor here are not about the mother and her power. They are about the woman and her power in that unattached way, which is the way of a person who is not defined by either marital status or progenitors.

What this Empress is about is the following: to do what needs to be done, regardless of how the public opinion happens to currently define gender roles. For instance, if this ruler is part of this trio, *The Hanged Man, The Empress & Raise,* we understand that the situation is about punishing the wicked and striking a deal with the rich, raising the stakes. There's no room for any other negotiation. In her seriousness, the Empress has her eyes on the radiant *Sol Niger,* the black sun of the Saturnian current, for this Venus knows her own worth.

The Hanged Man   The Empress   Raise

THE EMPEROR

The Emperor

A powerful man is seated between two tall pillars. From beneath his robe we can see his gesture: he gives. As no one is above him, the Emperor can afford to give. In traditional tarots we associate the card of the Star with giving, but I always wondered about that. Celestial bodies cast their rays on us because they can't help it. It's more interesting with the power figures who can afford to be charitable, who can issue commands that can benefit a whole country, or delegate and defend because they can choose to.

I think of all this when I see this Emperor's hands. We are not here with any holding of regalia, such as the orb and the scepter that we see the Emperor is holding in any of the Marseille type tarots and other similar Western renditions. We are here with an Eastern representation, which casts absolute power as a mystery. For instance, the imperial regalia of Japan consists of three sacred objects of mythical nature: first a mirror and a jewel used to lure the sun goddess Amaterasu Omikami from the cave where she had withdrawn, after having plunged the world into darkness. Then a sword. These objects are considered so sacred that not even the Emperor himself can see them, though possessing them assures him ascendance to the throne.

In *Baka Tarot* the Emperor I had in mind when I envisioned him has a commanding nature that can settle both the folding of the game and the ensuing retreat from the gambling table, if that is what it takes to maintain sovereignty. We see this in the trio of cards here: *Fold, The Emperor & The Hermit*. Power has a straightforward nature. The Emperor understands that, and so does his posture and his gaze.

HIGH PRIESTS

High Priests

When I thought of what the most exciting part of being a High Priest is, I immediately thought about exorcisms. In most cultures there's the social function that priests perform that has to do with comforting, giving spiritual guidance, and officiating at weddings and funerals. But there's the other, and more interesting, aspect of the job that some would call esoteric or occult. This part is about trafficking with spirits, vanquishing demons, performing acts of 'uncrossing' if bad luck is registered, and writing grimoires. Sunday sermons can be quite clever, and reciting from the Book of the Dead can also be quite fascinating to listen to, but the crafting of a rite that has the potential to make your hair rise is of another order.

What you see in this card is not just one, but two priests tending to the Devil who, although singularly represented in *Baka Tarot*, also makes an appearance here. The High Priests act in accordance with what we expect of them. But what of the Devil? Is he not a High Priest too? If we're to go with the biblical text, no one is more versed or more proficient at quoting from the scripture than the Devil. That alone qualifies the Devil as clergy, even as we think of consecrations. How about this one: 'Speak of the Devil, and he doth appear.' Is this act not an act of consecration already?

I don't want to put words into your mouth, as that would be contrary to what I teach, namely, that all should rely on their own cultural competence and ability to read a visual text when looking at any tarot cards, but I'll just say this, by way of pointing and asking: what do you make of the zigzag line that goes from the eyes of the priest on the right to his hand? If you think 'zapping,' you're on the right track.

If this card shows up in your readings, think of all manners of being zapped, a lower order of electrocution, and less than being struck by lightening. The zapping energy of this priest goes through his sleeves into the Devil's ear. Now try to make something out of this image, also as the idea may apply to this trio of cards, *High Priests, Force & Fold:* a forceful zap, and the Devil folds.

High Priests   Force   Fold

THE LOVERS

The Lovers

In most historical tarots the Lovers card depicts this situation: a young man is caught between two women and we presume that he needs to make a choice: 'this one or that one?' Meanwhile, Cupid shoots his arrow rendering the Lover's indecision irrelevant. It turns out that, when it comes down to it, it's not the man who makes a choice. Fate does, and the man submits to it.

So this card, traditionally speaking, is all about pretense, as 'the choice' is not the result of 'free will,' nor is it the result of doing what one likes. Rather, 'the choice' is nothing but a display of an actual lack of agency.

But let us turn the tradition around, and introduce the seducer, *femme fatale*, into the picture, the dreaded 'other woman,' notorious for breaking up marriages. What kind of a lover is she? You'll notice that in *Baka Tarot* the Empress makes a trip to the Lovers card, where we find two, smaller figures, a young man and a woman, sharing an intimate embrace. The Empress, dressed up in her finest garb, is watching the two, and one can almost hear her say, '*baka,* such stupid love...' Her mind projects a halo around the two lovers, like a spell, as if suggesting that whatever the young lovers are doing, it will not last long.

Perhaps this is her reaction to the kind of young men who are drawn to her, only in the end to reject her with these words: 'you're already taken.' While this lover may be 'a married queen already,' her status has nothing to do with her agency. In her own perception, the strong, beautiful, and rich woman is a free agent. In love no one possesses anyone, even if the contrary is claimed by popular agreement, as the person in love makes no choices at all. When in love, one shares one's own infinity.

But sure, if *The Lovers* card shows up in your readings alongside with other cards such as *Judgment & Check*, you can dispense these words of wisdom to the one in doubt: 'you may hear the call, the Piper's enchanted song luring the innocent and not so innocent to forbidden places, but if you check your place in relation to the other players, you may get a clear sense of your role in the expectation that you must belong to someone other than yourself. If belonging is not for you, then act in accordance.'

Judgment   Check   The Lovers

THE CHARIOTEER

The Charioteer

n *Baka Tarot* the Charioteer card is all about 'the man and his horse.' Without a horse, no kingdom, though the man we see here is no ruler of any country. He is in service to the king, representing the king's power and interests.

On another level this is also a card about legs. Standing on two firm legs, to be more precise. The young man does it, and so does the horse. Standing upright they seem equal in size, though, obviously, if the correct perspective was observed, then the image of the horse here would have to be much bigger. But what interests me is how the horse's front legs come up against a scroll, as this is suggestive of the power that mediates between two other powers: horse power and warrior power. Without a script, so to speak, there's no proper communication between man and animal. How could there be, since each speaks its own language?

Some like to stress the power of the wordless communication between people and animals. There is such a thing, and one is welcome to ask me about it, since I like to think of myself as a great animal communicator. But it we have to be fair in terms of how we 'understand' what is going on, we cannot run to the 'intuitive' fountain for help. It helps us not. We may delude our-selves about getting it, but a delusion is still a delusion.

So what do we make of communicating with horses, the ones that can save our lives, in the process allowing us to play heroic parts and take the praise for it too? Say, you get this trio of cards: *The Empress, the Charioteer & The Wheel of Fortune.* As soon as we look at this string of pictures, we get it that we're with a different kind of ride here. When the Empress and her Black Sun made up of a murmuration of starlings approach, the horse gets spooked. But the warrior wants to show his worth. 'I'll turn this black dot into a wheel,' the young man may say, and before you know it, we're back to the Fool and his hula hoop.

Imagine the word '*baka*' used as a command to make your horse do as you instruct it. 'What goes around, comes around,' the Wheel also instructs, which leaves us speculating on what the Empress has to say about it. Will she lift her flowery skirt and instruct the Charioteer into the mysteries of what she is riding on, or with?

The Empress

The Charioteer

The Wheel of Fortune

61

JUSTICE

Justice

Justice is our lady of truth and method. In the rendition here, *Baka Tarot* style, Justice is not presiding over anything, sitting firmly on a throne and clutching her sword and scales, as she does in other standard tarots. No. Here Justice is moving about swiftly, like a ninja. In her hands we find the proverbial crystal ball mirroring a skull. For let's face it, who can ever know the truth? We might as well look for it in smoky mirrors and other reflective surfaces. Only the dead also speak the truth, they say. In court judges look at evidence, evidence, and then more evidence. While they do this, they also listen to all sorts of versions of truth. Subject to discourse, truth can be a colourful thing.

I thought of all this when I tried to imagine a ninja at work in intelligence, on the one hand collecting information, and on the other, spreading rumours, participating in sophisticated forms of 'truth construction.' For instance, there's nothing more entertaining than reading about Japan in the Sengoku period, the years between 1477–1573, when the warring provinces produced some of the most memorable historical figures, from generals to loyal samurai and diplomatic monks. Each had a notion of what justice was as a virtue and how it had to be executed as a law.

In *Baka Tarot* the ninja carrying the crystal ball of fate is a figure that distinguishes between the immutability of the law and the more fluid justice that dispenses fairness, all according to its own self-assuredness. If this sounds complicated, think of what basis people have for their beliefs, when they either cast truth in their own image or sanction its form according to what is convenient.

But let's look at *Justice* in context, being flanked by two other cards, *Fold & The Tower*. The calligraphist may pen down the law in accordance with what is decided. Lady Justice comes along, reads the writing on the wall, and passes sentence: 'off with their heads.' People get sent to jail, or they fall from grace. There's nothing here to be sentimental about. In this sense punishment is always divine. Can it ever be anything else? This question is the only form of a realized truth, the here and now that conflates the just with justice, and the concept of justice with its executioner.

Fold

Justice

The Tower

THE HERMIT

The Hermit

What is this? Some may ask, demanding an explanation. 'Does the Hermit need two lamps?' Here's the subtle answer: the extra lamp is in the picture to highlight the idea that the first and foremost function of the Hermit is to retreat from everything. Why such a radical take, retreating, that is? Well, think about it. Once we get old, is there anything that we need? There is nothing that we need. Not even a long and healthy life.

If you think really hard about it, regardless of how distasteful or dreadful this proposition may be, the reality of it is inescapable. So, no, the Hermit doesn't *need* two lamps. The only thing he needs, apart from the absolute nothing, is acceptance. Things are as they are. If the Hermit should ever doubt this, he could arm himself with two lamps, front and back for good measure. He can stare into each light, and start nodding at the realization that, when it comes down to it, he doesn't even need understanding. At an advanced age life may still be vexing, but will understanding what resists comprehension change anything about it? Like what?

It is this that the Hermit, if at all wise, should be after, the realization of truth, which is the same as the realization of now. The *now,* which is not even the present, is neither subject to change, nor subject to comprehension.

If the Hermit fails to see this, there's always someone in *Baka Tarot* who will help him get it. If *The Hermit* is flanked by *The High Priestess,* who is herself preceded by *Justice,* then he is in for a treat. These ladies don't have any time for the perplexed. One knows already what the truth is and the other can intuit it. All the Hermit needs to do is watch and listen.

Or, indeed, for once, if the Hermit must advance, rather than retreat, then he should do it by taking steps towards the woman, keeper of the book. If philosophy won't help him, she will.

Justice The High Priestess The Hermit

THE WHEEL OF FORTUNE

The Wheel of Fortune

I n most introductions to the tarot you come across the idea that the Wheel of Fortune is all about change. Fair enough, but what does a wheel do, before it represents change? It turns. This primary function of the wheel is often forgotten in the Anglo-American world, but as soon as we turn our gaze towards the East, the story is different. As the Wheel turns in all its manifestations, from enabling a car to functioning in a clock, it doesn't just represent change, but also momentum.

Our *Baka*, the Fool, sits atop the Wheel. If we go downwards to the right, we see him on his head already, looking like the wheel's lever. Imagine the Fool turning the wheel. But this happens to us all. Now we're up, and now we're down. There's nothing new in this. Knowing, however, when we're up and when we're down is not always a given. Sometimes we mix these positions. This often happens due to our clinging nature. When we're on top of the world, we think we'll just stay there. The Wheel may turn and we turn with it, and yet we can't see that our position has changed. This is called failing to see that the momentum in not with us anymore.

Of all the characters depicted in the trumps, the one who knows all about the momentum not being with him is *The Hanged Man*. If *The Wheel of Fortune* is nearby, he can hold his breath. I don't want to say, 'exhale,' since the Hanged Man is always in peril of exhaling for good, but he *can* hold his breath, for a new turn is in the picture. If *The Charioteer* pulls the wheel's lever, there's a good chance that the Hanged Man will ride again.

By virtue of impermanence, change is always here. But when it comes to the turning of the Wheel, I'd say that this event is contingent on other factors. Imagine the Charioteer sticking his whip into a wheel, just because he can, instead of using it on a horse. What then? When the Wheel of Fortune is in the picture, we must think of what fortune, precisely, turns it, as it's not the same as assuming that the Wheel changes our fortune.

In other renditions of this card we see a King sitting on top of the Wheel, awaiting his downfall. In *Baka Tarot* this place is reserved for the Fool, the *Baka* himself. That's because I like the saying that goes, 'Fortune favors the Fool.' This means that if the Fool comes down, his good fortune will follow, aiding him.

The Hanged Man

The Wheel of Fortune

The Charioteer

FORCE

Force

By the law of transposition,' we say, when we talk about dynamic images, pointing to how one element on a card can turn into another, especially if a rhyming scheme is noticed. In the story about the Wheel of Fortune, I showed how the Hanged Man's momentum changed. When the time was right for him, and he got untied and stopped hanging, he could hop on his horse and ride again. Applying the same logic of observation, we can also talk about strength and the conditions that either enable it or disable it. When strength is enabled it manifests as a magnetic power. When strength is disabled, we talk about forcing and resistance.

In *Baka Tarot* the Star woman visits a lion. This is an auspicious encounter. As a visitor, however, the Star doesn't outshine the lion, but we can talk about the right emanations towards it. While the lion exhibits a powerful look, the woman's radiance lends this look a magnetic force.

Consider this trio of cards, *The Empress, Force & The Star*. If the Empress emanates the Black Sun's power from her heart towards the lion, the lion in turn can become a whole constellation. In astrology the zodiacal sign Leo is ruled by the Sun, our most powerful star. While other stars in nearby constellations can also influence us, their force is less distinct. What we learn from emanations, however, is what style is all about: a way of being in the world that's finely calibrated to an individual expression. *Non serviam* may well be the motto of all stylish people.

The three women in our trio of cards here pack a lot of power. Each is aware of her function to the point of being stellar in performing it. The brilliance of each woman's performance is in her signature. When force is with us in its magnetic manifestation, there's no resistance that we cannot overcome. A disabled mode can be enabled again by wearing an insignia that says, 'this one has fortitude, and it shines.'

THE HANGED MAN

The Hanged Man

Sometimes I think I watch too many Japanese calligraphy masters engaging with performance art. One of their specialties is to get a hold of a whole white wall, and then swing their big brushes against it. Sometimes, very big brushes. They do their glyphs in a manner of seconds, and then watch as the whole design starts to drip. Drip, drip, drip. The lavishness of the ink fascinates me. I thought of the image of the Hanged Man being the result of brushes drenched in ink and then splattered all over a wall. Something will hang for sure. But we don't know which part will stand out the most. Not that standing out is the most important, but from a performative point of view, the spectacular has grit.

We tend to think of the Magician in the tarot as being the foremost representative of staged theatrics, but how about the Hanged Man? To my knowledge no one has ever addressed the power of the spectacle in the Hanged Man's performance, which is mostly involuntary. Still. Back in history criminals would be punished by being drawn and quartered in the town's square. People would gather to watch the spectacle. Acts of lynching and hanging would also draw the crowds, as any form of punishment carries a certain element of entertainment with it.

Traditionalists like to associate the figure of the Hanged Man with the idea of being able to see things from a different perspective, what with hanging upside down, the suggestion also being that this inverse seeing is somehow something that the Hanged Man himself desires. But that is a misunderstood idea.

In *Baka Tarot* the Hanged Man is subject to involuntary elongations of his limbs, to his regret. As a result, he will see the world differently, for sure, but it will have nothing to do with his own will. In fact, this card speaks of complete lack of agency. When hanged, the only option is to hang in there and wait for rescue, or to simply expire. There's only so much dripping a hanged body can produce. When dripping stops, life stops.

In context, if *The Hanged Man* appears alongside with the cards of *The Fool & Raise*, we get the distinct idea of loss. The Fool has no problem raising the stakes, but if this will be done on a day when fortune doesn't favour him, all he will get out of it is an unfortunate hanging.

DEATH

Death

I wanted Death to have a defiant look: 'Look what I can do, take heads. When I swing my scythe, heads are rolling.' That's real power. In fact, when we think about it, can we think of someone who is more powerful than Death? Like who, or what? In contrast to death, we tend to think of life as being powerful, and perhaps *the* most powerful, but is that so? If death decides to take life, who is going to stop it? No one and no thing. Death *can* have a defiant look, for it is entirely justified.

What is also connected to the power of death is the idea that with death everything is final. There's never any room for negotiation here. Not even for the benevolent notion that death means transformation. Another misunderstood conception.

In some folk traditions we can come across stories of people who get to extend their lives by making a pledge. Another bizarre belief that seems to me to be a manifestation of wishful thinking, as in this speculation: 'we can cut a deal with the Devil. Why not Death?' Then the arrogance of thinking that we, somehow, can defy Death. How? Death is the ultimate defiant. I say, no thanks, to any other well-intended illusion.

In a reading, if we get this trio of cards, *The Wheel of Fortune, the Magician & Death,* we may see this arrogance in play. 'Look at me,' the Magician may say, 'I can make entire cities vanish, turn wheels that are stuck in a pattern of the eternal return of the same, and cheat Death.' Death comes along and says nothing. The only thing we hear is the swishing of the blade.

In this encounter Death gestures towards the Magician, 'you talk too much.' When I say this I don't mean to imply that Death actually uses words to accompany the gesture. Rather, what I mean to say is that Death speaks through a presentation of bones. Even cloaked, Death will show its own ribs. We may be allowed to count them. But I think that it would make Death happier, if we just stuck to counting the skulls it takes, instead or taking stock of how its own deadly countenance appears. This will make us appreciate the old dictum, *memento mori,* more.

The Wheel of Fortune   The Magician   Death

TEMPERANCE

Temperance

There's something to be said about the virtue of Temperance, especially as far as we imagine it. Formal, not so formal; dressed, yet quite undressed; drunk, but also sober. As far as I'm concerned, this card is not just about keeping things in balance, which is a popular view, but rather about containing multitudes. To make this idea more concrete, think of it this way: if the Magician can hold as many ideas in his head as we can possibly imagine, Temperance is about their embodiment. And then moderation, calibration, and reverberation.

The latter attribute here is not added as a mere alliterative trick. Rather, the notion of reverberation is conjured here as an invitation to think about resonance. That's what Temperance is all about in my not so humble opinion. When Temperance makes a cocktail, she holds in her right hand the ingredients of the 'left hand path.' Without the secret of the *pharmakon,* drug and poison taken together, there's no magic cure. Temperance is also our snake charmer; her naked bosom, the promise of heaven. The glass itself into which she pours her medicine mirrors the illicit refinement that Temperance stands for.

This great alchemist wears two sets of wings. One for her night time excursions into poisons, and another for actual flight towards angelic visions. Under the influence, however, we can do more than just see green stars. We can intone to the *abracadabra* on the wall, tap the floor with legendary Aaron's stuff, taken straight out of the Bible, and reverberate.

You wouldn't necessarily think of *Temperance* as a force that can bind, but if we find this lady between *The Magician & High Priests*, we'll be right there with the magic of hexing, crossing, and uncrossing. The Magician says the word, Temperance recalibrates it by making permutations with the word, and the High Priests perform the rite. Whichever rite, or whatever it takes to get the job done. Whichever job. If it resonates, it works, and if it works, that's all you need to know.

THE DEVIL

The Devil

Quotations. 'Speak of the Devil, and he doth appear,' I said earlier in my description of the card of the High Priests, when I proposed that this conjuration is an act of consecration. When *The Devil* is flanked by *The Moon* and the card of *Call,* we can rewrite the old maxim and say, 'call on the Devil, and the creatures of the night shall appear.' If we said this, we would be performing a reading from right to left, which is not always the most usual way of going about it, as we're mainly prone to reading from left to right, following our Latin alphabet. But when the cards fall on our table in this way, then it's almost a given that we start with the imperative, 'Call.' And so we do.

Generally we refer to the Devil quoting the Bible as an act of reading inversely, an act whose function is to twist the sacred words so that they become intentionally profane. In some witchcraft circles the inverse reading is mirrored in the recitation of the Lord's prayer backwards in order to commit to what opposes the dominant religion of Christianity, in the process alluding also to making a pact with the Devil for the purpose of renouncing the promise of salvation that we find in the Bible in exchange for knowledge or a different kind of gnosis that allows us to know ourselves first, before we believe in anything anyone else has to say.

As I'm not fond of promises myself, and I'm all for the Greek injunction, 'know thyself,' I find all these discursive inversions befitting my own style of engaging with the so-called occult arts. In *Baka Tarot* the Devil's chest sports a pair of lungs filled with calligraphy, glyphs that recall the *abracadabra* on the scroll. And no, this figure of the Devil is not a stylized bat taken straight out of the Romanian folklore that traffics with all things demonic in this image... say I, in an act of denegation.

You see, this is exactly the Devil's work. To see the words, say them, and then negate them. I don't want to call on Freud, so that *he* shall appear, but he was on to something when he insisted on theorizing so extensively on denegation, or denial raised to the power of two-fold vibrations. Take that as you will. If I were to say more here, I'd have to call it 'A New Black Mass,' and I'm not sure that the *Baka* would like that very much.

THE TOWER

The Tower

As we speak of the Devil, so we speak of the Tower. But in terms of aims, whereas the first is invoked for unexpected appearances that we subconsciously desire, the second works with the hand of fate, as we don't normally conjure a natural catastrophe. When the lightning strikes, it strikes independently of what we want or don't want.

In most traditional renditions of this card, the Tower gets struck, fire catches its top, and from there, disaster, the first manifestation of it being involuntary evacuation. Some images dramatically portray desperate people throwing themselves out of the flaming tower, in hope of a better fate than burning. But alas, if the tower is tall, falling from its height has equally fatal consequences, the only difference being that while burning alive can take longer, in the case of a fall, death can occur instantaneously. So we're here with a choice between two evils.

One would think that since the Devil card precedes numerically the Tower card, we are done with the demonic, but this image tells us that there can still be more of it. In *Baka Tarot*, however, we are with a modified image of the inevitably impending devilish death, or the image that conjures symbols of separation: from divorce to simply moving out of the tall building, even if the latter may be more of a representation of eviction than the choice to change addresses.

In *Baka Tarot* while people fall from grace, they also find another, if hitting the ground is not fatal. The two most distinct figures falling are now on a slope, dancing, while an intact tower in the background just above them offers them a new chance. So, indeed, not all that goes down the drain, or burns to ashes, leads to misery. Sometimes a catastrophic event leads to an opportunity for a more intimate *pas-de-deux,* or a tango.

In this trio of cards, *Justice, The Tower & Temperance,* we see an image of rehabilitation. It may well be that the court decides that one's address should be in jail, but after the time spent there, the situation can re-balance. Or else, the force of natural lightning is not subject to opinion. If it happens, it happens. If one survives the strike, one may find shelter in a pub. Imagine the counsel from an angelic bartender, while she pours you a much needed drink. You can always take it from there.

THE STAR

The Star

f we look up at the starry night on a clear evening, we cannot help but be in awe. It's hard to conceptualize it, but we're here with an infinite bursting of light. The very thought of the infinite starry universe is enough to induce a sense of vertigo in us. Who can grasp this mystery?

In *Baka Tarot* I was interested in depicting this burst of light and how we might capture it in an emblem. In astro-magical circles this emblem is called a talisman, the object that is crafted with view to drawing down the power of a particular star. I'm grateful to the ancients and, more particularly, the Chinese and Arab astrologers, who came up with the idea that this is possible. Imagine capturing the power of Aldebaran, Sirius, Algol, or Spica in a pin or in a coin that features the story of this star's 'intelligence.' Imagine talking about astro-intelligence in the first place. Enough to make your head spin.

The Star woman here carries her talisman on her bosom: a star mirroring the bursting universe. We're not just with metaphors here, but also metonymy. In this relation a celebrity is a star and the star the whole universe. Metaphorically speaking we lend the stars human agency: the stars are guides, helping us navigate. Stars are also watchers. They can wink too. Stars can peek from behind the clouds, hanging from the sky.

Let's see what metaphor we can activate, if we see this trio of cards, *The Emperor, the Star & Call:* a powerful man is turned on by the star of his calling. I like that. I like the idea that although we may already sit comfortably on it, that is to say our vocation, there is, as yet, more we can discover about our infinite potential. Power is all the greater when it's aligned with recognition, or the realization that we each perform what we are called to perform. The Emperor makes his wish upon a Star, emanating his will, The Star registers it, and The Fortuneteller encapsulates it in her crystal ball, sealing the fate and saying: 'it is your call.'

THE MOON

The Moon

We associate the moon with imagination. From poetry to schizophrenia, from illusion to delusion, and from deception to romance, the moon can take it all. In fact, since we're with such a wide range, why not two moons? In most popular renditions of this card, we already find the theme of two, from the Marseille tarot, where we have two dogs howling at the moon at quite some distance from the two towers in the city, to the Waite/Smith tarot featuring the same.

We can see one moon, but we can also imagine another right next to it. Why must two dogs howl at the same moon? Can't they each have their own to dream of? I thought I'd make a card with two moons in it, in the same way that I thought the Hermit could have two lamps.

'It is like the finger pointing to the moon...' This is Bruce Lee speaking in the film, *Enter the Dragon,* as a variation on the saying that 'if we can think it, it exists' — a variation with a deconstructive twist, as we are here with Zen Buddhist teachings, famous for not settling on what appears to be so. Nothing is just so.

We find this analogy of the finger pointing to the moon central to understanding how our mind works. When we point to the moon, do we see our finger pointing, do we see the moon independently of the finger pointing to it, or do we completely misunderstand what the light of the moon is all about? We can't settle this. The two dogs here can't settle this either, hence the suggestion that they might as well mind their own solitude.

What is a world of dreams for one dog is a bright sun for the other. This trio of cards, *The World, The Moon & The Sun* suggests that much. What can be perfectly clear for one, can be equally obscure for the other. As a famous linguist put it, 'all communication is miscommunication' – though he may also have been under the influence of the *Shurangama Sutra's* finger and moon dilemma, when he said that.

It's a good thing that in *Baka Tarot* we have quite a number of crystal balls that diverse characters can look into. We can suspend our disbelief, and dream about what the other is thinking. As we will never have access to another's mind, we might as well go with projection. We call this entertainment.

The World   The Moon   The Sun

THE SUN

The Sun

When everything is illuminated, there's no worry. At least that's one of the many benefits that clarity can have for us. When everything is illuminated, we can be on the same page as others. When clarity rules, there's no other world view, no forcing, or resisting that can trump it. I get this idea when I look at this trio of cards, *Force, The World & The Sun*. When all is well, it ends well. When mutual respect rules, the world of man and animal can come together without grief or dominance.

In *Baka Tarot* we have two suns for good measure. We follow the rhyming scheme established with the Hermit's two lamps and the two moons on the Moon card, and say the following: if the Moon is a powerful attractor of perplexing ideas, the Sun gives form to the conceptual, or the philosophy behind the world of ideas. This applies to the reading of visual material in this way: 'once you see it, you can't unsee it.' The strength of a reading is not in proclamation, as words can ruin everything. Rather, the strength of a reading is in the ability to attract what is obvious, what is clear.

Why is this important? Think about relationships. If you can't read the other properly, make that, brilliantly, you'll end up with the moon situation, having a depressed view of what you can barely comprehend. The emanation of light from the sun reminds us of our job, which is to make ourselves attractive of the light of the other we wish to communicate with. It's not about seeking to understand another person's mind and motivations. It's about attracting their strength, so we can end up taming all the beasts.

As our sun is the closest star to us in our constellation, it reminds us of the obviousness of all existence. We attract light by default. Without this light, there's no life. I wanted to highlight this attracting power when I added a second source of light on the cards that carry two primary symbols. We can dream twice as hard with two moons, philosophize twice as profoundly with two lamps, and love another twice as much with two suns. With our lights on, as it were, our stamina in the world can only grow stronger and our magnetism unbeatable. Others call this being successful at life.

Force   The World   The Sun

JUDGMENT

Judgment

A ll rise,' I want to say, whenever I see the card of Judgment, and then I remember, 'we're not in court here.' But language has that ability to lock us in habitual patterns. We hear what we want to hear. In traditional tarots, in addition to the angel of Temperance, we see on the Judgment card yet another angel blowing into a trumpet.

In *Baka Tarot* we're with a figure from theatre, traditional Japanese Noh theatre, orchestrating both the void and what we expect is music coming out of a primitive clarinet, or a *shakuhachi*, a flute made from bamboo.

I introduce these foreign words here to suggest that when we rise to a new consciousness, our language changes, and we get accustomed to hearing new tones and idioms. So if there's any transformation that we can talk about, I'd say it is found in this.

The lovers in the Sun card make an appearance here, though if you notice, their bodies and hair look slightly different. Since any resurrection presupposes death, it is to be expected that if a rising from the dead occurs, the old shapes will now be transformed.

We're with the world of an orchestrated stage here, led by sound yet again, but perhaps not as loud as we'd expect from a card that features none other than the sounds of the Final Judgment. Here, whoever blows into the clarinet, conducting with it too, pleases the crowd. Two people are more distinct. Above the two behind the orchestrator is a ghost taking shape. This is because I always thought when looking at various Judgment cards that I was missing seeing the ghosts in action. If the idea is to raise the dead, can we, at least, have a sense of their arriving?

Perhaps we're with passing judgment here, after all. What happens when we read this card in context? Let's look at this trio, *The Lovers, The Fool & Judgment.* Two women and one man. A man who turns into a Fool. Why this transformation? Because the choice was wrong? Indeed, there is such a thing. You make the wrong choice, and you rise to a new life. If you're lucky, you'll enjoy the new tunes and language games. If you're not, you'll be struggling like a ghost to take form. As they say, embodiment is not for everyone. Or wait. I think I said that myself somewhere, in another life.

THE WORLD

The World

Under the watchful eye of the moon, the distant sun, and the even remoter planets, the world is dominated by water. Out of the swirling ocean, the ultimate ninja fortuneteller emerges with her crystal ball, prophesying declaratively in Zen style: 'the world is what is the case,' echoing also philosopher Ludwig Wittgenstein.

This ominous figure may well look like another Venus in one of Botticelli's paintings, a woman revealing her beauty inside another sea creature, the oyster, and she may even recall the nymph in the mandorla in most traditional tarots, the half naked being protected by a wreath of greens and the four zoomorphized evangelists. But…

If the idea of protection persists in *Baka Tarot*, we find it in the spell, in the asemic writing rendered throughout the deck, the wordless open semantic form of magic, cousin to the more symbolically loaded nonsense we find in *abracadabra* and the key of keys directive, *open sesame*. Micro and macro worlds come together in this card, the reading of each being enabled by the capable eyes of the surfing fortuneteller.

We are not with nakedness in this card, as the world itself is not naked to the perceiving eye. The world being what is the case is never naked. It is informed by both sentient awareness and utter ignorance. 'What are we here for?' ask the Zen masters rhetorically, for the answer is already a given. Once we're done with pointing to the moon, in the process finding ourselves perilously enamored in our finger, we realize that we're forever with the flow. Even when we go against it, or resist it, we're still with the flow. Whether coming or going, we're with the flow.

In mundane operations, if we come across the cards of *Check, The Lovers & The World,* we may dispense instant advise: 'Check your involvement in other people's affairs. Instead of meddling, you may want to use the same wave you're riding on, the same one that brushes the lovers feet, and yet keep going, keep gliding. A world of magic awaits you beyond the anguished pathology of love, a world of spells cast for the sea, the sun, the moon, and other stars, spells locked in your crystal, the mirror of your own true justice, the justice that says: desire stops here. Taste the salt of the earth that tastes you.'

CALL

Call

The fortuneteller in this deck is a conjuror. If 'the world is what is the case,' armed with a crystal ball, the conjuror conjures worlds beyond the world. Worlds that most people have a hard time believing in. Not that these worlds can or should be subject to beliefs, most of them petty beliefs, but still, it's the fewest who are willing to go beyond, beyond formal seeing, social constructions, habits, childhood traumas, problems. But the faceless conjuror here has another agenda than transacting with beliefs. She is into calls. She is into the business of just doing it. Her own name takes after the action she performs, 'Call.'

Calling is an interesting event. At the casino we call, especially when we don't believe the other's hand. Through calling we conjure into existence the other person's luck or, as the case is often, their misfortune. We call on others when we want to visit. We call spirits into bottles that we can then seal for a specific purpose. We call on forces that are unseen. In *Baka Tarot* a cute ghost is willing to come forth. Although most Japanese are afraid of ghosts, they'd probably think of the small figure appearing here as being *kawaii,* having a friendly disposition. But with ghosts you never know, though you can go deeper with the spirit calls, as no one can prevent you from calling their bluff.

In divination settings, the poker actions can be very useful. Since they're all commands, there's nothing to think about here. You get this card, call. No matter the context you may be sitting with, you can always just call. If *Call* is on the table alongside with *High Priests & Raise,* you can almost sense the heightened energies in place. High Priests have a reputation for being able to fix the stakes, especially the raised ones.

But there's always a winner, a hand that's more powerful. Sometimes you have to risk your own luck, if you want to see great fortune in action. No stake is ever too high for that. Look into your conjured worlds, and discern. Luck begins there, with a call.

CHECK

Check

The chips on the casino table have the same value. The slight tap on the cards to check also has the same value. In the context of gambling, chips and taps are about waiting. While the chips are waiting to be taken, the taps signal waiting for another round of bids. You'd think that waiting is a static event. But not in gambling situations. Watching the pros take possession of the chips on the table or anticipating taking them through a tapping gesture that indicates waiting for another round of bids discloses a very dynamic play at hand. Some gamblers get their full body in swing when they play, the better of them demonstrating great control even of the way their hair moves around.

A finely choreographed play is a pleasure to watch, as the money taking game becomes a performance towards the declarative precision of 'the winner takes it all.' Gaming is about giving and taking, the aim being to calibrate the game so that taking comes at last, or is the last move.

How do we apply what we see in gambling games to reading cards? Let's go straight for it, and plunge into a fortunetelling scenario. Let's play the 'question and answer' game based on this trio of cards: *Check, The Charioteer & The Hanged Man.'*

Question: 'My partner has offended me. What attitude is best to embody in light of this situation?'

Answer: 'Check with his motivation. It looks like his strong drive got the better of him. But acknowledge also that the momentum is not with you. You must let it all hang. You got two waiting cards here, so it's best to wait it out and not overreact. The offence won't go away, and you will still feel like punishing him, which you may too, as per what we do with traitors, but since you're advised to check, then check. Wait for another round, and then see if it's still necessary to act as a punisher. Suspend your anger. Hang it on a peg for the time being, and wait for the right moment to have another go at it.'

When this card appears in your readings, consider all manners of waiting, checking, biding your time, and reading the room, especially in their differentiated forms.

Check   The Charioteer   The Hanged Man

RAISE

Raise

We're not with the Wild Wild West in *Baka Tarot* in terms of imagery, but we're not far from the idea either. The only difference here from the 'anything goes' attitude characteristic of the Wild Wild West is the composed countenance of the Man in Black. Whoever can say, 'raise,' must have a winning hand, one way or another. By this I mean that when we raise the stakes, we do it because we can afford it, either financially or psychologically.

If we haven't been dealt just the cards, but have just the mind that can manipulate the other players, we are in business. Whether we raise hell or heaven is of no consequence, as each of these places are on a par in relation to our stamina. If we have it, not only can we do anything, but we can also endure everything. A strong stamina is a superpower.

I'm thinking of the necessary strength that goes into projecting that kind of power, the raising power, when I look at these cards on my table: *Force, Raise & Judgment*. We can relegate force to some external source, for instance when we say, 'may the force be with us,' thus entrusting our fate to the hand of fortune. But we can also think of strength as a magnetic power we already possess. We may not always know how to tap into it, but if we apply fortitude to our courage, chances are that we may discover what our stamina is made of.

I don't share this insight, however, with the person I'm reading the cards for, as their question is related to something else. 'What will I gain if I accept this man's proposal of marriage?' a woman wants to know. 'If not everything,' I tell her, 'then a lot of power. The way you will move in the world with this man will feel like Judgment Day, having the nature of a great awakening. The union will be so forceful that it will make a great impact. If impact can be thought of as something to be gained, then this marriage will be useful to you.'

Some predictions sound too good to be true. Others make us consider the risks of their dominant power. For although people never do what you tell them to do, most of them love a dictation. But if the fortuneteller says, 'Raise that hell or heaven,' people listen up, sensing a power that roams in mysterious ways.

Fold

ometimes you are called to put an end to it, fold it,' I tell the person I'm reading the cards of *Call, Death & Fold* for. A straightforward sentence based on clear imagery. In the context of design, in *Baka Tarot* the Fold card represents the calligraphist. When I first got into the art, what fascinated me the most was the speed of the brush. And the paper. You can draw a circle in less than a second. Imagine that. A perfect splash of ink made in less than a second. Sometimes I wonder: in this day and age of productivity and countless coaching towards it, why isn't anybody referring to calligraphy as a source for it? No one is more productive than a calligraphist. Perfect too, as scribbling without the intention to edit must be the most rewarding of acts. One we could all emulate in our perennial seeking of secret recipes that will unlock our productive powers.

But this card here is not about that. Nor is it about ridiculing our stupid endeavors. *Baka,* all the way... This card is about knowing when to put a full stop to whatever we're doing. When is enough, enough? What will give us a sense of that?

It's lucky with the tarot in general, as the whole pack is really nothing but a tool for prompting based on endless permutations with the cards. Is there another tool for better thinking, thinking with yourself, really, than the tarot? I can't think of it. Every time three cards hit my table, a new story emerges. Call, kill it, fold it. That's it.

When that is said, I hope no one using this tarot will ever ask me about the agony that goes into the other kind of thinking, if not the devilish kind, then most certainly the stupid kind, the *Baka* kind, related to my very un-Zen squirms about ruining a perfectly fine piece of handmade Japanese paper. Why do I always think in terms of ruining it, rather than in terms of embellishing it? What nonsense possesses me? Secretly I entertain the idea of my most cherished Zen masters approving of my attachment. 'Just fold it,' they would then say. 'Put it all down,' and I'd go, 'all? What is all?' But you see, this question is my trick towards postponing putting a full stop to it. Goddammit. I'm not a master calligraphist, in spite of ruining many good papers with my ink. But how I wish I was one…

THE DEAL

Cards are for dealing. Whether we play games with them, tell fortunes or divine with them, cards are meant to be shuffled and dealt. What makes it interesting is the hand we get. Who can ever get tired of seeing what awesomeness randomness gives us? Not I. I love this game of cards, and because I do, I want to see others get excited about it, hence this project of sharing the *Baka Tarot,* when sharing was not even in the picture to begin with. But here we are.

You can no longer get a copy of the talismanic limited edition *Baka Tarot,* unless you're lucky to find someone who will want to part with theirs. But you *can* get the standard cards. If you go to my website – www.cameliaelias.com – and consult the Art section there, you will find a link to where you can get the cards. As this was an *ad hoc* project and I didn't want to make a big fuss about publishing the cards and the book together, and then have the pleasure of stocking the set under my bed, taking it out to distribute it myself whenever an enthusiast would happen upon it, you will have to make the effort to get the cards and the book from the different sources that manufacture each.

While the book is published by EyeCorner Press for global distribution at various online stores, from Amazon to Barnes and Noble and others, the cards are published by MPC, and can be purchased directly at my *Read Like the Devil* store with this company. Here are the relevant links:

MPC
https://www.makeplayingcards.com/sell/readlikethedevil

EYECORNER PRESS
www.eyecorner.press

Now go get 'em, the cards and the people you want to read for. I hope you have great fun with this tarot, and in the process experience what a calligraphic journey is all about, namely the expediency of being in the moment and catching a glimpse of the forever elusive and impenetrable obviousness that surrounds us without letting us see it. If you can make a deal with someone other than the Devil, namely yourself, a deal to see what there's to see, then you're in for surprising discoveries.

Milton Keynes UK
Ingram Content Group UK Ltd.
UKHW051523271223
435058UK00003B/5